FAST CARS

PORSCHE

by Lisa Bullard

Reading Consultant:
Barbara J. Fox
Reading Specialist
North Carolina State University

Content Consultant:
James Elliott
Editor
Classic & Sports Car magazine

Capstone
press

Mankato, Minnesota

Blazers is published by Capstone Press,
151 Good Counsel Drive, P.O. Box 669, Mankato, Minnesota 56002.
www.capstonepress.com

Library of Congress Cataloging-in-Publication Data
Bullard, Lisa.
    Porsche / by Lisa Bullard.
    p. cm.—(Blazers. Fast cars)
    Includes bibliographical references and index.
    ISBN-13: 978-1-4296-0104-7 (hardcover)
    ISBN-10: 1-4296-0104-3 (hardcover)
    1. Porsche automobile—Juvenile literature. I. Title. II. Series.
TL215.P75B85 2008
629.222—dc22   2007005676

Summary: Briefly describes Porsche history and models.

Editorial Credits
Erika L. Shores, editor; Bobbi J. Wyss, designer; Jo Miller, photo researcher

Photo Credits
Alamy/Phil Talbot, 12–13
AP/Wide World Photos/Porsche AG, 4–5, 6, 15 (bottom), 21
Corbis/Bettmann, 8–9, 14 (bottom); Car Culture, 28–29; Kenneth James, 18;
    Peter Harholdt, 23 (top)
Getty Images Inc./Bongarts/Christof Koepsel, 7
Rex USA/Tony Kyriacou, 11, 14 (top)
Ron Kimball Stock/Ron Kimball, cover, 15 (top), 16–17, 23 (bottom), 24–25,
    26–27

Essential content terms are *bold* and are defined at the
bottom of the page where they first appear.

1 2 3 4 5 6 12 11 10 09 08 07

TABLE OF CONTENTS

chapter 1

EVERYDAY SPORTS CAR

Cars, SUVs, and trucks cruise down the freeway. One hot sports car catches every eye. A stylish Porsche stands out in a crowd.

Speedy Porsches shine on the race track. But Porsche also makes **production cars** for everyday driving. Porsche drivers say their cars are more reliable and comfortable than other sports cars.

production car — a vehicle produced for mass-market sale

Porsche Carrera GT

Porsche Carrera Cup race

fast fact

The Porsche Carrera GT, built from 2004 to 2006, is a supercar. It can reach a stunning speed of 205 miles (330 km) per hour.

chapter 2

SPORTS CAR FAME

Ferdinand Porsche started the Porsche company in Germany in the 1930s. The company released its first production car, the Porsche 356, in 1948.

In 1964, Porsche's most famous car hit the streets. The 911 has a rear-mounted engine. The air-cooled engine of the first 911 produced 148 **horsepower**.

horsepower — a unit for measuring an engine's power

fast fact

Porsche continues to improve the 911. The company sells 13 different 911 models today.

The first front-engined Porsche hit the streets in 1975. At first, the Porsche 924 was supposed to be a Volkswagen. Porsche bought the design and added its own features to make it a Porsche.

fast fact

Ferdinand Porsche also helped create the Volkswagen Beetle. The first Porsches used many Volkswagen parts.

PORSCHE TIMELINE

Production begins on Porsche 911.

1964

1948

1974

The first 911 Turbo is released.

Porsche 356 is introduced.

A smaller and less expensive Porsche began production in 1996. More drivers could afford the Porsche Boxster convertible. It cost nearly $30,000 less than some Porsche models.

Porsche Carrera GT is released.

The Porsche 911 Carrera 4 hits the streets.

1988

2004

1996

Porsche Boxster is introduced.

chapter 3

TURBO-CHARGED

The 2007 Porsche 911 Turbo is the most powerful 911 on the road. Two **turbochargers** push the car to a top speed of 193 miles (310 km) per hour.

turbocharger — a system that forces air through an engine to make a car go faster

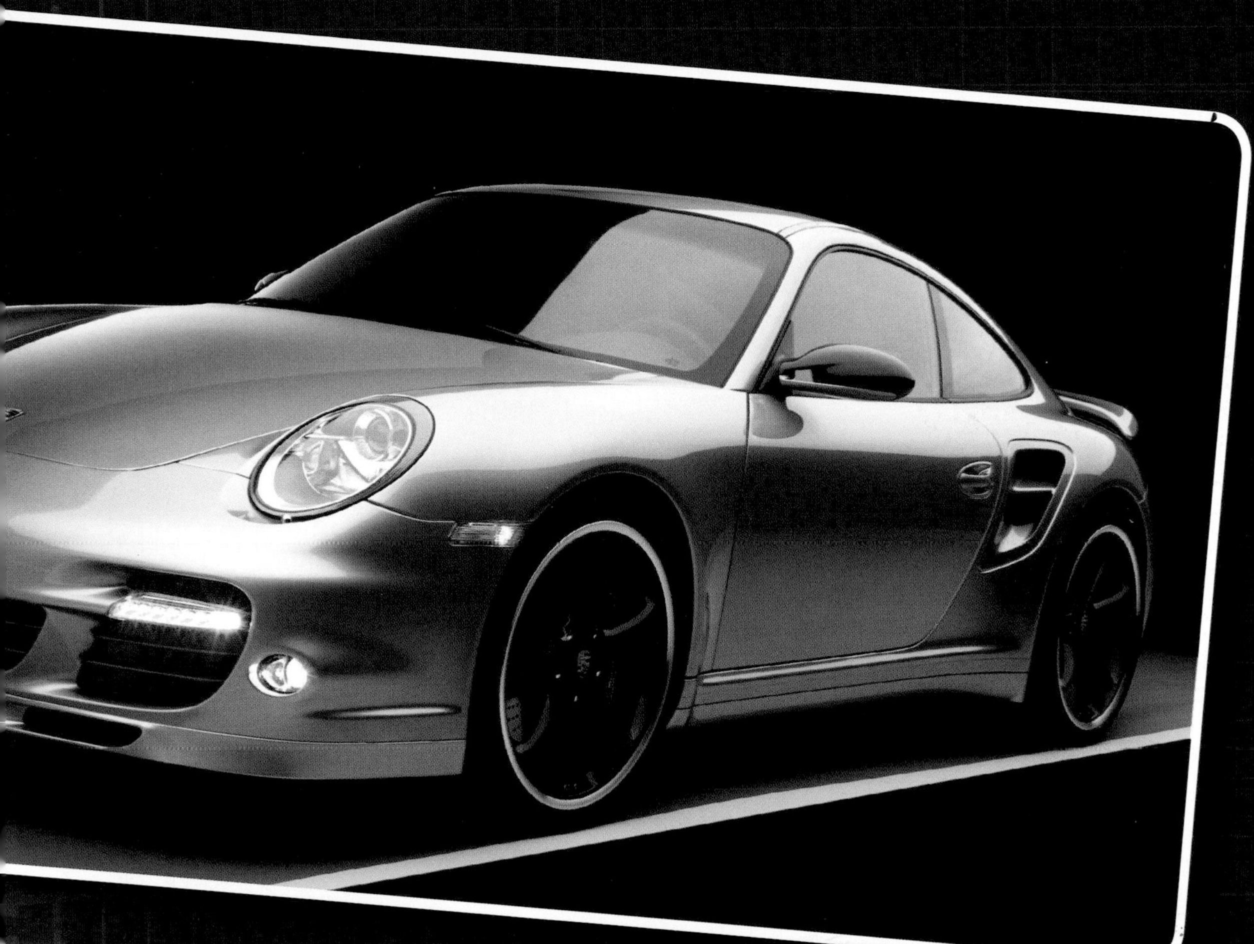

The 911 Turbo is also known for its massive brakes. At 60 miles (97 km) per hour, the car comes to a complete stop in 99 feet (30 meters) with a touch of the brakes.

fast fact

The Porsche 911 Turbo speeds from 0 to 60 miles (97 km) per hour in 3.7 seconds.

The Porsche 911 Turbo zooms flawlessly through every turn. A system in the car keeps track of driving conditions. The system decides whether to send more power to the front or back wheels.

fast fact

Porsche 911 Turbo owners can pay more than $120,000 for their superfast cars.

SOMETHING OLD, SOMETHING NEW

Porsche is always adding technology to improve its cars. But the Porsche 911 look hasn't changed much over the years. It still has its famous teardrop shape.

1980s Porsche 911 (top)
2007 Porsche 911 (bottom)

Porsche added a new rear **spoiler** to many of its cars. The spoiler lies flat until the car reaches 75 miles (121 km) per hour. Then the spoiler pops up to keep the car from lifting off the road.

> **spoiler** — a wing-shaped part attached to a sports car that helps improve the car's handling

PORSCHE DIAGRAM

hood ornament

Xenon headlight

magnesium wheel

bumper

chapter 5

LOOKING AHEAD

Today, Porsche builds other fast road machines, including the Cayenne sport utility vehicle. But nothing is likely to top the fame of the Porsche 911.

GLOSSARY

feature (FEE-chuhr)—an important part or quality of something

horsepower (HORSS-pou-ur)—a unit for measuring an engine's power

production car (pruh-DUHK-shuhn KAR)—a vehicle produced for mass-market sale

reliable (ree-LYE-uh-buhl)—trustworthy and dependable

spoiler (SPOIL-uhr)—a wing-shaped part attached to a sports car that helps improve the car's handling

technology (tek-NOL-uh-jee)—the use of science to do practical things, such as designing complex machines

turbocharger (TUR-boh-char-juhr)—a system that forces air through an engine to make a car go faster

READ MORE

Hawley, Rebecca. *Porsche.* Superfast Cars.
New York: PowerKids Press, 2007.

Kimber, David. *Auto-Mania.* Vehicle-Mania!
Milwaukee: Gareth Stevens, 2004.

Stacy, Lee. *Porsche.* Hot Cars. Vero Beach, Fla.:
Rourke, 2007.

INTERNET SITES

FactHound offers a safe, fun way to find Internet sites related to this book. All of the sites on FactHound have been researched by our staff.

Here's how:
1. Visit *www.facthound.com*
2. Choose your grade level.
3. Type in this book ID **1429601043** for age-appropriate sites. You may also browse subjects by clicking on letters, or by clicking on pictures and words.
4. Click on the **Fetch It** button.

FactHound will fetch the best sites for you!

INDEX